Priceless Penny

by
Lauren Kramer-Theuerkauf

Illustrated by James Sell

"Today is the day," thought Penny excitedly.

It was adoption day at the shelter and she just knew that she was going to find her forever home.

She had spent all night dreaming about what sort of family she would be adopted into.

Would there be children to play with?

Maybe a big yard to run around in?

The doors of the shelter burst open and soon, people began to fill the room.

Penny had taken great care to look her best. She sat straight up in the cage and flashed her prettiest smile.

A man approached, peeked in and walked away.

"Strange," thought Penny.

"Maybe he'll come back."

Next, an elderly woman shuffled up to her cage.

She peered at Penny through her thick glasses and shook her head.

"That poor little thing," she said as she made her way down the aisle.

A family with two little girls appeared.

"What's the matter with its leg?" asked the father gruffly.

"Penny was born this way," Ann, a shelter volunteer explained.

"Ew!" cried the girls. "We don't want her!"

Penny was placed back into her cage.

"What is wrong with my leg?" Penny pondered.

She couldn't figure out what had just happened.

Just then, two teenage boys walked by.

"Whoa!" said one boy. "Look at this freak!"

"That is one ugly dog," said the other.

Penny could not believe it!

She was.....ugly?

"That leg is so weird!" they went on.

"And check out that super long tail."

"Yeah, and those ears look like satellite dishes."

"What a loser!" they shouted and walked away.

Penny felt horrible. She didn't feel any different from the other dogs...but maybe she was.

Adoption day drew to a close and Penny found herself still in the shelter.

"Maybe I won't ever be adopted," she sighed.

Two days later, a woman came into the shelter. She stopped in front of Penny's cage.

"Oh my goodness!" the woman exclaimed.

"She thinks I'm ugly," thought Penny as she watched the woman walk away.

For the next few days, Penny felt depressed.

Why couldn't she be more like the other dogs? Why did she have to be so different?

Then, Penny heard a familiar voice. It was the woman from earlier in the week!

"Penny," said Ann, "you are about to go on an adventure."

Soon, Penny found herself being placed into a van.

The driver smiled at her as he closed the door and sped off.

The journey continued for days.

Finally, they arrived at a place called Second Chance Animal Rescue in Springfield, Illinois. Penny then met her foster mom, Sherri.

Living at Sherri's house was a dream come true. There were even other dogs to play with!

One day, Sherri and her friend Cynthia loaded Penny into a car.

"Where are we going?" a frightened Penny wondered.

She worried that she would be dropped off at another shelter where she would be alone.

Sherri rang the doorbell and waited. The door opened and a woman appeared.

"Is this Penny?" she asked.

Penny did her best to keep her long tail tucked and her ears laid back. But what could she do about her paw and snout?

"It sure is," said Sherri.

"She is priceless," said the woman.

"Hello, Penny. I'm Lauren and I am going to be your new mom."

Penny immediately began to look around.

"This seems like a nice place," she thought. "And that couch looks comfy,"

Taking a huge leap, Penny landed perfectly on the cushions.

"Did you see that?" Lauren cried.

"We had just assumed that because of her paw she would need extra help."

"Oh, Penny can get around just fine," said Cynthia. "She can do everything that a four legged dog can do."

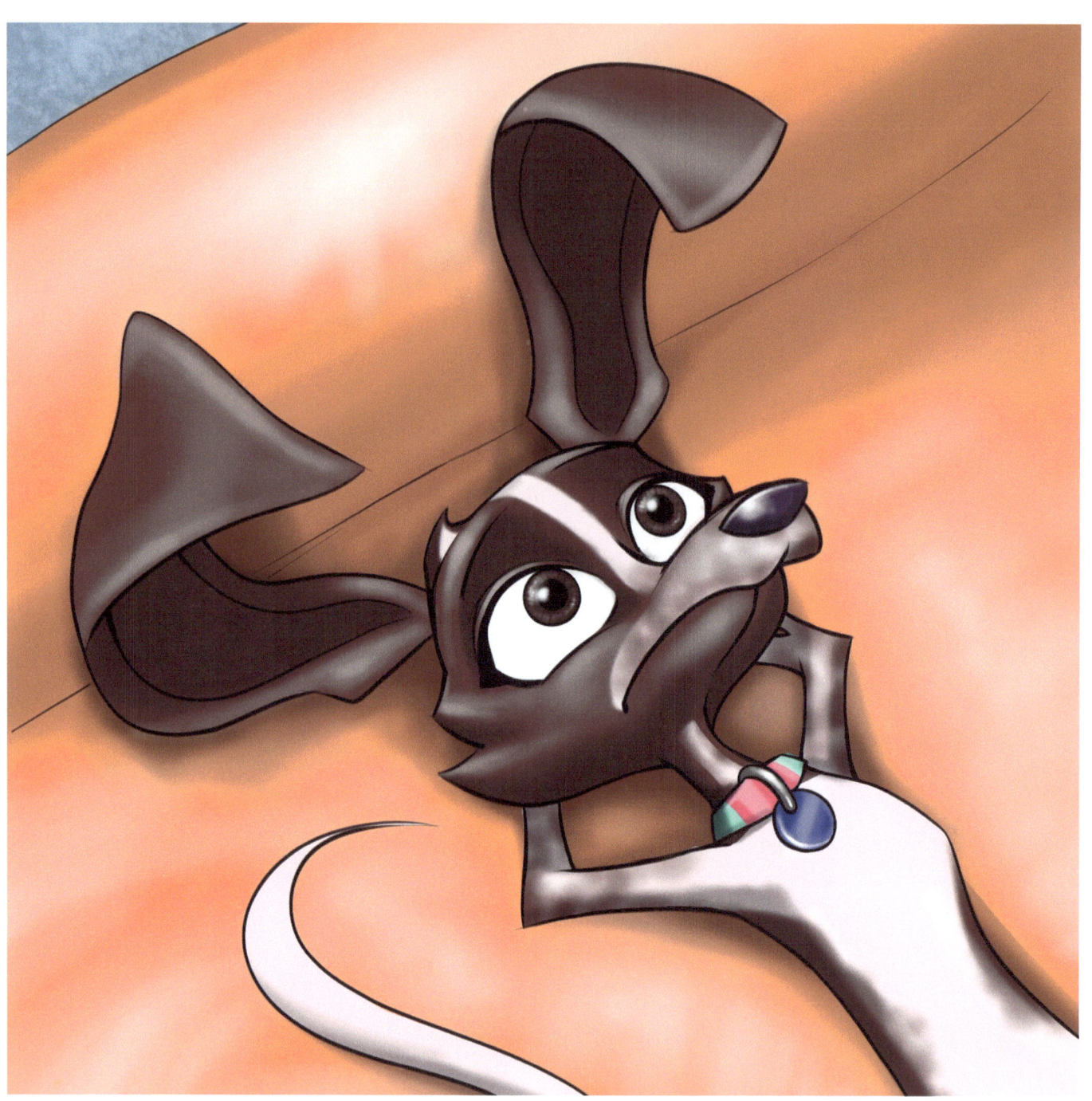

"Should we see how she does with our other dogs?" Lauren asked.

"Other dogs?" Penny gulped.

What would the other dogs think about her? Would they make fun of her?

The first dog that appeared was a long haired Chihuahua named Theo.

He stared at Penny then slowly made his way over.

Penny sat frozen as Theo sniffed her special paw...and licked her nose!

She then met Adriel, another Chihuahua. Penny couldn't help but notice that Adriel's tongue was sticking out, right at Penny!

"Her tongue is actually longer than her head, so it always sticks out. She was born that way," Lauren explained.

"Born that way?" thought Penny. "Just like my paw!"

Next, Penny met Domino.

He was black and white but his eyes were as blue as the sky.

Then there was Cole.

He was much bigger than Penny but for some reason she wasn't afraid.

She hopped over to him and he gave her a big, sloppy kiss and then began chasing her around the room!

Penny was so happy!

Not only was she being adopted, but she was going to have four furry friends to play with.

And a family who loves her.....just exactly the way that she is.

These are the faces of rescue.

Please adopt your next furry friend from your local animal shelter or rescue group.

Together, we can show the world that
different is *beautiful!*

About the Author

Lauren Kramer-Theuerkauf began writing at an early age. While in elementary school, she was the recipient of two Young Author Awards (1994, 1997). She received a Bachelor of Science degree in Mass Communications-Print Journalism from Southern Illinois University Edwardsville. While there, she earned the Outstanding Student in Journalism award in 2006. Kramer-Theuerkauf is also an active member of the Society of Children's Book Writers and Illustrators (SCBWI) and the Independent Book Publishers Association (IBPA).

Priceless Penny is the second book written by Kramer-Theuerkauf.
Her first book is a collection of poetry entitled *More Than Words* that was published in 2010. Lauren currently lives in Freeburg Illinois with her husband, Matt, and their five rescue dogs and two cats.

James Sell is a published children's book Illustrator and freelance graphic designer for CartoonsandPortraits.co.uk. He has worked as a concept artist for character design and development for BAFTA nominated children's TV and film studio 'Absolutely Cuckoo'. He has since directed and produced storyboard and concept work for the children's charity 'Change of Scene'. James studied Graphic Design, Illustration and Animation at the Reigate School of Art, Design and Media where he was awarded Best Animation in 2007. Shortly after, James won a national advertising competition for Esure Insurance, awarded to him by copywriter Chris Wilkins. He now lives in Horley, England and continues to pursue his passion in creating charming illustrations.

www.ingramcontent.com/pod-product-compliance
Lightning Source LLC
Chambersburg PA
CBHW041539040426
42446CB00002B/150